THE CARABAO-TURTLE RACE

and Other Classic Philippine Animal Folk Tales

A TREASURY OF PHILIPPINE FOLK TALES

THE CARABAO-TURTLE RACE

and Other Classic Philippine Animal Folk Tales

as told by SYLVIA MENDEZ VENTURA

Illustrated by JOANNE DE LEÓN

Tahanan Books for Young Readers

MANILA

Published by Tahanan Books for Young Readers
A division of Tahanan Pacific, inc.
P.O. Box 9079
MCS Mailing Center
1299 Makati, Metro Manila
Philippines

Book design and line-drawings by Beth Parrocha
Printed in the Philippines by Rapid Litographics and Publishing House
1 3 5 4 2

National Library of the Philippines Cataloging-in-Publication Data

Recommended entry:

Ventura, Sylvia Mendez.
    The Carabao-turtle race
and other classic Philippine
animal folk tales / Sylvia
Mendez Ventura. - Makati,
Metro Manila : Tahanan
Books for Young Readers,
c1993. - 56 p.

    1. Fables, English -
Philippines. I. Title.

PN989P5 1993 398.245 P931000005
ISBN 971-630-016-6

Contents

Introduction

There is a sign in a zoo. It is on the glass window of a cage that houses a small sleeping snake. The sign reads: "Please do not tap on my window. How would you like it if I banged on *your* window and woke *you* up?"

The message to the visitor is clear: Try to understand how animals feel. They are very much like you.

In the relationship between human beings and animals, nothing stands out so starkly as the behavioral analogies between them. Who could ever forget Aesop's fable of the dog carrying a piece of meat and barking at his reflection in the water? Or La Fontaine's fable of the hard-working ant and the happy-go-lucky grasshopper?

Human speech abounds in images and allusions to animals familiar to the average child. A brave person fights like a lion; an athlete swims like a fish; a gossipy person is catty; the big bad wolf is an enemy to be kept from the door. Mother Goose is a bespectacled bird in bonnet and apron, spinning her verse-stories in the comfort of her rocking chair.

Our kinship with animals is the foundation not only of the fables children read in school, but also of Rudyard Kipling's *Jungle Book,* Disney-inspired animated cartoons and comic strips, Dr. Seuss's Cat in the Hat, and Hollywood's King Kong. Zoological fiction continues to flourish as a literary genre, universal in time and place, enjoyed by adults and children alike.

The eight animal stories in this book are retellings of selections from *Filipino Popular Tales,* collected by the eminent American folklorist Dean S. Fansler. The originals appeared in print for the first time in 1921, when the American Folk-Lore Society published the anthology.

Fansler compiled the tales during the years between 1908 and 1914, when he was teaching at the University of the Philippines. The stories were part of a rich oral tradition before they were set down on paper by Fansler's students.

To show that the tales were *bona fide* native stories, and to indicate their geographical distribution, Fansler gave the name of each narrator and his/her native town and province. He wrote interesting notes comparing varieties of a particular plot as narrated in different regions or provinces, citing analogous tales in the folk literature of other countries, and speculating on the possible origin of some Philippine tales.

Fansler observed that the story of the monkey-turtle rivalry is widespread in the Philippines and could have descended from Buddhist fables; that the monkey-crocodile encounter has parallels in Chinese, Swahili, Japanese, and Russian folk tales; and that racing and flying competitions among animals occur in the talking-beast tales of different cultures.

In the form recorded by his informants, Fansler's tales are hardly more than sketches and are not child-oriented. They are, however, rich in possibilities for expansion of plot, character development, local color, dialogue, and onomatopoeia.

Folk literature travels with ease from one storyteller to another, and I am only one in a long line of writers trying to give new life to old tales. I have changed titles, invented situations, and given proper names to the major characters based on what they are actually called in either English or Tagalog, such as Pagong for turtle, and Matsing and Mr. Unggoy for two different monkeys. I have given Mr. Buwaya a wife.

Except for the mother hen who lost a necklace, all the animal characters in the original tales were males. In fairness to the female of the species, I have transformed a number of males into females, such as the turtle in "How Pagong Made a Fool of Matsing" and the small bird called Coling in "The Bird that Reached the Sun." My alterations in title, situation, and gender have not affected the basic patterns and motifs of the originals.

I have aimed at a subtle balance between entertainment and edification. The outwitting of large animals by small ones in the so-called trickster tales is a source of suspense and amusement, even as it suggests the evils of vanity, selfishness, and the oppression of the weak. Death is the well-deserved fate of the greedy monkey Matsing, but the other monkey, Mr. Unggoy, earns our sympathy because he is the potential victim of a crocodile with murder on his mind.

Folk tale merges with myth in some stories such as "The Hawk's Rubies." Although its implied lesson could be "Neither a borrower nor a lender be," the story performs a mythic function by explaining why hens scratch and peck the ground and why hawk and hen are enemies. "The Ink Spouts" belongs in the realm of myth because it traces the origin of the black liquid secreted by the squid and the cuttlefish. At the same time the child could also read in the squid story the unpleasant consequences of being late and of abusing one's fellowmen.

The ultimate value of these classic animal tales is threefold. First, they make Filipino children aware of their cultural heritage. Second, they mirror the problems, imperfections, and foibles of human beings who must devise strategies for self-preservation and the improvement of their lot. Third, the diversity of animals who play their roles in these miniature dramas reminds us that the animal kingdom is a vast kingdom and that humanity is only a very small part of it.

Sylvia Mendez Ventura

The Carabao-Turtle Race

One summer morning Carabao was strolling, *gadong, gadong, gadong,* on a dusty country road. He was looking for water with which to wash the mud off his back. Just then he met Turtle crawling, *kimi, kimi, kimi,* from the rice field beyond.

Turtle wanted to be friends with Carabao. He thought big animals could be helpful in times of trouble. He had often seen Carabao walking with a rice bird and two flies perched on his back. "Any animal who lets other animals ride on his back must be a kind animal," thought Turtle.

"Hello, Carabao, how are you today?" said Turtle, poking his head out of his shell.

"I feel hot as a fried egg," answered Carabao. "Can you show me to the nearest pond? I could use a bath."

"There's a nice pond but it's quite far from here," said Turtle. "I'll be happy to show you the way."

"Just tell me where it is and I'll find it," said Carabao. "Is it under a siniguelas tree? Or under a banaba tree? Is it a small pond? Or is it big enough for me? You know I'm one of the biggest animals in the kingdom."

"Let me show you the way so you won't get lost," said Turtle, trying ever so hard to be friendly.

Carabao only laughed. "I'm in a hurry," he said. "If I let you lead the way, I might spend the next five days on the road."

Turtle's feelings were hurt. "I only want to help you," said Turtle, trying to hold back his tears. "I even thought we could be good friends and hunt for food together."

Carabao laughed even more. "What have I to do with creatures your size?" he snorted. "You'd be better off hunting with Snail than with a big, strong animal like me! And I'm a fast runner."

"Are you saying I'm as slow as Snail?" asked Turtle. He tried to raise himself on his hind legs but he fell over backward, *kaplunk,* on the dusty road.

"Exactly," laughed Carabao. "You and Snail are the slowest animals on earth because you each like to carry your house on your back. That's dumb, if you ask me!"

Turtle got back on his four legs and dusted himself off. "Listen, I can run faster than you any day," he blurted out.

Carabao could hardly believe his ears. "Humph! I would like to see you try that," he said.

"Then get ready to race with me," dared Turtle.

At first Carabao turned down the challenge. All his friends—Cow, Bull, and Horse—would surely laugh at him if they saw him in a contest with a foot-dragging turtle. "No, I won't race with a poor weakling like you," said Carabao, and he began to walk away.

"Very well," Turtle called after him. "I shall travel all over the kingdom and tell your friends and mine that you're no match for me. You're a coward."

Carabao stopped in his tracks. "I am not a coward," he declared. "All right, just to please you, I'll race with you."

"Will you race with me over three hills?" asked Turtle.

"I'll race with you over seven hills," boasted Carabao. He really thought Turtle was the silliest creature he had ever met.

"All right, seven hills will do," agreed Turtle.

"Just give me three days to wash up and invite my friends to watch the race," said Carabao as he turned to leave.

Turtle was glad he had three days to plan. That night he called seven of his turtle friends to a meeting. "Do you want to help me beat Carabao?" he asked.

"Yes!" they cried. "For the sake of the Turtle Club!"

So Turtle asked his friends to split up along the seven hills, one turtle per hill. He told them what to do and say.

On the day of the race, Carabao and Turtle met near the first hill. Palaka the frog was chosen to judge the contest. He gave the signal—

KOKAK!—and off they went.

Carabao raced as if he had all the time in the world, *ho-hum, gadong, gadong, ho-hum.* He stopped to talk with his friends. He paused to look at the leaves on the trees and the flowers along the way. He counted butterflies. Turtle, in the meantime, plodded along, *kimi, kimi, kimi,* under the noonday sun.

Carabao and Turtle soon lost sight of each other. Carabao believed Turtle was two kilometers behind him, trying to push his feeble body over the pebbles on the road.

Carabao ambled lazily to the top of the first hill. To his surprise, Turtle was there first, resting under a flowering gumamela bush. Turtle began jumping up and down, *hoopah, hoopah, hoopah,* and shouting, "Here I am, slowpoke!" Then Turtle disappeared down the hill, *kimi, kimi, kimi.*

"How could this happen?" wondered Carabao. He trudged down the first hill and up the second. Again, to his amazement, Turtle was on the hilltop—*hoopah, hoopah!*—yelling, "I'm here!"

"Impossible!" thought Carabao. But this time he decided not to walk too slowly. He began to trot, taking big steps. But when he reached the third hill—*hoopah!*—Turtle was already there, giggling, *"Tee-hee-hee."*

"No, no, this can't be!" cried the carabao, dashing to the fourth hill. As he was galloping up, *uh-guh, ug-guh, ug-guh,* he heard a familiar voice at the top, *"Tee-hee-hee."* Not only was Turtle there, he was actually swimming—*slosh, slosh, slosh!*—in a tiny pool of water.

And the same incredible thing happened over and over. When Carabao reached the top of the seventh hill, *uh-guh, uh-guh, uh-guh,*

Turtle was already there—*hoopah!*—ahead of Carabao.

The race was over. At the finish line Palaka held up Turtle's front leg and shouted, "The winner!"

Carabao lost his temper, *grr-uff, grr-uff, grr-uff!* How could he have been beaten by the slowest four-footed animal in the world? He got so angry he kicked Turtle Number Seven so hard that the turtle flew in the air and landed—*boiing!*—on a rocky patch of ground. But because every turtle has a tough shell, Turtle Number Seven was not at all hurt. In fact it was Carabao who cried in pain, *"Hati, hati, hati!* My foot, my foot!"

When Carabao looked at his foot, he saw that his hoof had been split in two.

And that is why all carabaos have split hooves.

How Pagong Made a Fool of Matsing

One morning Pagong the turtle and her friend Matsing the monkey decided to go fishing together. They sat on the river bank for many hours but no fish came close enough to get caught.

At about noontime they spied a leafy banana stalk floating by. Matsing had a bright idea. "We should be planting bananas instead of fishing!" he said.

"I was thinking of the same thing," said Pagong. "Why don't you reach for that banana stalk?"

Matsing's arms were long but they could not reach the stalk. It was floating away pretty fast.

"Why don't you get it, Pag?" asked Matsing. "You're a good swimmer."

Pagong said, "Yes, but only if you promise to split it in two—I'll keep the leaves and you keep the roots."

"It's a deal," agreed Matsing.

So Pagong dived—*swoosh!*—into the water to get the banana stalk. She gripped it with her teeth and hauled it to shore.

Matsing split the stalk into two parts with his bare hands. Then he looked at the large green leaves and thought to himself, "*Hmm-mm....* I like these. They look healthy and ready to bear fruit."

So he said to Pagong, "It was not easy to cut this stalk. Look, my hands are bloody." He showed Pagong his red palms. "I think *I* should get the leaves."

"But, Mat! You promised!" cried Pagong, stepping on the leaves to keep Matsing away from them.

But Pagong was too weak to fight Matsing. She watched sadly as her old friend grabbed the leaves and scampered off into the jungle.

Pagong found a nice spot in the woods to plant her black muddy roots even though she thought nothing would come of them. At the same time Matsing planted his fragrant green leaves. *"Yuk, yuk, yuk!"* chuckled Matsing as he dreamed about the tasty yellow bananas he would soon harvest.

To Matsing's great disappointment, the leaves turned brown and dry. *"Ugga, ugga, ugga!* These leaves are rusty! They must be dead!" he grumbled, swatting the leaves with his hands.

Meantime Pagong got the surprise of her life. Her black muddy roots grew into a beautiful stalk with glossy green leaves. One morning a purple heart blossomed from the stalk. After a few days the heart opened, showing rows and rows of pale purple flowers inside. Each flower turned into a green banana, which then ripened into a yellow banana. There must have been fifty bananas in all!

Word got around that Pagong was the proud owner of a blooming banana plant three meters tall. When Matsing heard the news, he swung through the trees in a hurry, *fwing, fwang, fwing*, to visit his old friend. He found Pagong helplessly staring up at her bananas, unable to pick them.

"Hello, Paggie!" smiled Matsing. "What's new?"

When Pagong saw Matsing, she forgot her anger. She knew Matsing was the only one who could help her. She said, "Mat, I'll give you half my bananas if you climb the stalk and pick the fruit for me."

"With pleasure," replied Matsing, walking nimbly up the stalk. Soon he was sitting in the middle of a leaf cluster, eating one banana after another, *yummy, yummy, yummy*.

"Here, Pag, have a banana!" he laughed, dropping the peelings on the ground. He made no move to come down and share a single banana with the turtle.

Pagong drew her head into her shell and grit her teeth in anger. "*Ngit, ngit, ngit!* I'll teach him a lesson," she muttered.

While Matsing was busy munching away among the leaves, Pagong collected ten pointed sticks and stuck them in the soil around the base of the banana stalk.

Then Pagong started shouting, "Here come the hunters! Here come the hunters!"

Matsing was terribly afraid of hunters because they killed animals. He slid down the stalk as fast as he could. Poor Matsing! The sharp

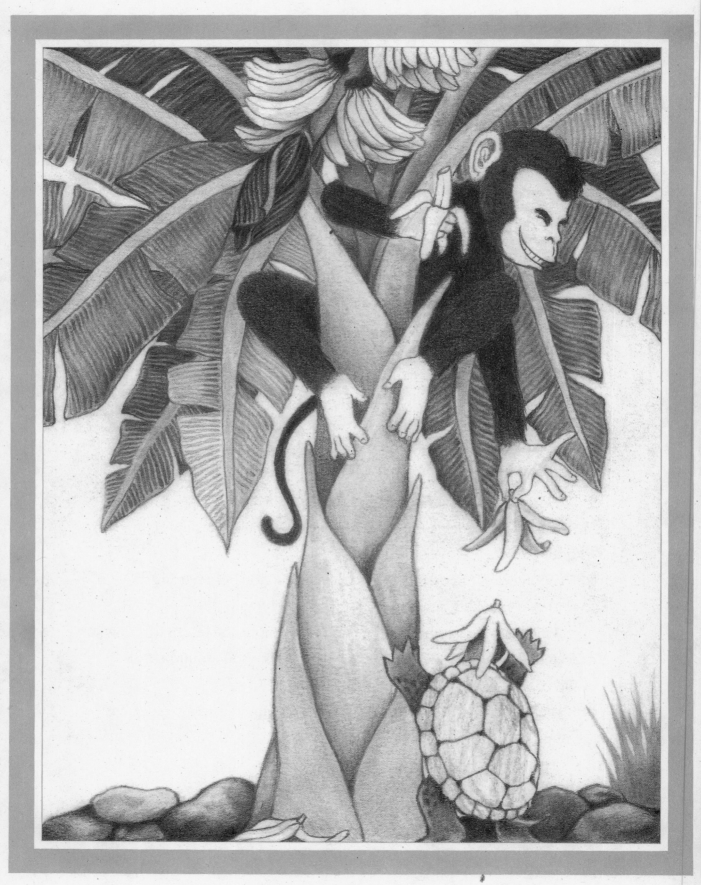

sticks pierced his body and he died.

Word of Matsing's death quickly spread to the Monkey Village. Soon Pagong was surrounded by a crowd of angry monkeys.

"This villain has killed a *matsing!*" they shouted. "Arrest her!"

Pagong tried to escape but before she could even hide her head in her shell, the monkeys were upon her. They tied a wire around her neck and dragged her upside down over rough stones, *tug, tug, tug,* to the palace of King Monkey. There Pagong was tried for murder and found guilty.

"Burn her to death!" ordered King Monkey.

"*Gooti, gooti,* I don't mind fire at all!" laughed Pagong. "See this red mark on my back? My father burned me there many times when he was angry."

"In that case," bellowed King Monkey, "don't burn her! Chop her to pieces!"

Pagong only smiled. "*Tee-hee, tee-hee,* cut me up if you like. See the scars on my shell? My father used to cut me up every day. Then I glued myself together again."

King Monkey shouted to his soldiers, "*Ahoo!* What shall we do with this criminal?"

"Throw her in the lake!" yelled the soldiers.

When Pagong heard this, she began to shake in her shell, *katok, katok, katok.*

"*Ayeee!* Please, please don't throw me in the lake!" she pleaded. "I don't want to drown!"

"To the lake with her!" commanded King Monkey.

The soldier monkeys dragged Pagong to the nearest lake. All the while, Pagong was begging them—*ayeee, ayeee*—not to punish her in such a cruel way.

When they reached the lake, the monkeys raised Pagong in the air and—heave-ho!—they hurled her into the deepest part. Pagong landed—*loo-bog!*—in the water and disappeared.

The monkeys clapped their hands. They thought Pagong was gone for good.

Suddenly, who should stick her head above the water but Pagong herself, bubbling with laughter, *"Ngee, ngee, ngee!* Thank you, dear friends, for sending me home!"

The Bird that Reached the Sun

Lawin the hawk was the swiftest bird in Ibonland. Some days he flew so high that he could hardly see his own nest on the cliff. He also bragged the most. He liked to make fun of birds smaller than he, like doves and quails. He liked to challenge them to a race. Whenever he beat a bird in a race, Lawin would laugh and say, "Why don't you stop flying and try swimming instead?"

One day, having nothing better to do, Lawin flew around Ibonland, *zoom, zoom, zoom*, looking for birds to race with.

"Come here, Maya, and race with me!" he called out.

Maya tried to race with Lawin, only to feel her tiny wings wilting after five minutes. The farthest she could reach was the top of the macopa tree. There she sat for the rest of the day, too tired to fly another inch. Lawin,

21

in the meantime, swooped and soared and went into a tailspin without getting tired.

"What about you?" said Lawin to Flycatcher. "I bet I could fly faster than you!"

Poor Flycatcher. He could fly no higher than the flies he caught for his dinner.

"Haw haw!" laughed Lawin, spreading his majestic wings and pretending to be an airplane.

Once he saw Woodpecker pecking holes in the trunk of a narra tree. "Do you want to race with me, Woodpecker?" asked Lawin.

"I'm too busy," answered Woodpecker, *peck, peck, peck.* This wise bird knew he was no match for Lawin. He preferred to spend his time boring holes.

One day Lawin chanced upon a little black bird he had never met before. Her head was crowned with thick black feathers. She was sitting on the branch of a guava tree, nibbling ripe guavas with her tiny beak.

Lawin landed on a nearby branch. The guava tree shook as if a storm wind, *whooo, whooo, whooo,* had blown through it.

"Who are you?" asked Lawin curiously.

"My name is Coling," answered the little bird, between bites of ripe guava.

"How would you like to race with me, Coling?" said Lawin.

Coling looked at Lawin's huge wings. She knew she would never win a race with such a big bird. But Coling had a clever plan.

"Of course!" replied Coling. "When do you want me to race with you?"

Lawin was delighted that he had a new rival.

"Whenever you please. Me, I'm always ready to beat any bird in flight," boasted Lawin.

"Tomorrow before sunrise," suggested Coling. "But each of us must carry something to make the race a little more difficult."

"Well, this is a strange kind of bird," thought Lawin. Aloud he asked, "What do you want to carry?"

"I will carry some salt," replied Coling. "And you?"

"I will carry some cotton," answered Lawin.

The two birds agreed to meet on the branch of a breadfruit tree the next day. They asked Uwak the crow to judge the race.

Lawin laughed, *heh, heh, heh*, all the way to the cotton field. "What a light load I'll be carrying," he said to himself. "Lighter than a piece of paper."

Coling flew, *wing, wing, wing*, to the sea and collected a bag of salt. It looked quite heavy for such a teeny-weeny bird.

The next morning, before sunrise, the two birds met at the breadfruit tree. All the other birds were there to watch the race. Of course all bets were on Lawin to win. Nobody bet on little Coling.

Uwak gave the signal: "On your mark, get set, *WAK!*"

In a second Lawin and Coling were airborne—*zip, zip!*—faster than a pair of jet planes.

At first Lawin flew faster and higher than Coling. "*Heh heh!* That's what you get for carrying so much baggage!" he laughed as he watched Coling struggling upward, *oop, oop, oop*, with her salt.

Then something surprising happened. *Pitik, pitik, pitik.* Lawin felt

something wet on his head. "What's this?" he wondered.

It was beginning to rain! At first it was just a drizzle. Then it began to rain in big drops, *patak, patak, patak.* Lawin's ball of cotton was soaked with water. "*Ay, ay, ay!* My wings are getting too heavy," he groaned.

Coling's salt also got wet. But instead of getting heavier, the salt melted. When all the salt had melted, Coling felt as light as a feather. She flew, *wing, wing, wing*, as high as Lawin.

"How are you doing?" asked Coling merrily, flitting back and forth in front of Lawin.

"*Yug, yug, yug*," panted Lawin under his load of wet cotton.

"Goodbye!" cried Coling as she shot up so high that Lawin could no longer see her. "I've won the race!" cheered Coling.

What a wonderful feeling! The rain had stopped and Coling saw a rainbow arched across the heavens. She loved the colors—red, blue, green, yellow....

Suddenly she began to feel terrific heat all around her, *eee-neet, eee-neet!* Then she saw a huge red ball of fire hanging in the sky. It was the sun!

Too late for Coling to avoid it! The sun had burned the thick feathers on her head. *Krrak, krrak, putok!* Before the flames could reach the rest of her body, she made a crash dive into a puddle below, *ee-ee-ee-ya-bung!*

"*Haw haw!*" laughed Lawin triumphantly when he saw Coling falling. He dropped his bag of cotton and flew to Uwak. "I won the race!" announced Lawin.

The birds clapped their wings for the champion, although the smaller birds felt sorry for poor Coling. Uwak got the trophy ready for Lawin.

Just then, to everyone's surprise, Coling came along, *fililit, fililit, fililit.* Her wings were slightly wet but still fluttering.

"*Yawk!* I thought you were dead!" yelled the astonished Lawin. "You were all aflame when I last saw you!"

"I won the race!" declared Coling. "Look at my bald head! I flew all the way to the sun and got burned. Lawin didn't even reach the rainbow!"

The birds studied the evidence. Sure enough, the feathers on Coling's head were gone. Only a smooth bald spot remained, like the round bald spot on the head of an old monk.

So Coling was crowned High-Flying Champion of Ibonland. Lawin flew away, his head hanging in shame at his defeat.

Since that day, Coling has worn her bald spot like a medal, in memory of the day she beat the mighty Lawin.

Mr. Buwaya and Mr. Unggoy

Mr. and Mrs. Buwaya lived in a mangrove swamp on the bank of a river. Mr. Buwaya was quite a lazy crocodile. He loved to lie in the sun all day with his eyes half-shut. Sometimes his wife would whack him with her long tail just so he would move and do something to make life more exciting.

One evening, while husband and wife were having supper, Mrs. Buwaya complained, "I'm tired of eating river frogs. Go get me a monkey's liver for supper tomorrow night. And make sure it's a big one."

"Yes, dear," promised Mr. Buwaya. He, too, was tired of the same old food day after day.

The next morning Mr. and Mrs. Buwaya woke up bright and early.

They had a tasteless breakfast of earthworms in cold water. Then Mr. Buwaya glided out of the swamp, *whoosh*, and into the river.

"Don't forget what I told you last night," Mrs. Buwaya reminded her husband, waving goodbye to him with her long tail.

Mr. Buwaya was in a cheerful mood. He had a feeling he would find a monkey with a fat liver. He had often heard monkeys chattering, *chitti, chitti, chitti*, somewhere in the jungle. He had also seen banana peelings floating down the river. So he was sure there was a monkey village nearby.

After cruising for about twenty minutes, Mr. Buwaya spotted a monkey named Mr. Unggoy standing on the river bank. He was carrying an empty basket and was wondering how he could cross to the banana grove on the other side.

Mr. Buwaya paddled close to the bank and greeted Mr. Unggoy: "Good morning, sir. May I help you?"

"Good morning," replied Mr. Unggoy happily. "Can you ferry me to the banana grove on the other side of the river?"

"Gladly," replied Mr. Buwaya. "Just hop on my back."

Mr. Unggoy hopped on the crocodile's back, *plop,* and sat down with his basket on his lap. "It's a nice day," the monkey remarked, looking up at the cloudless blue sky and the coconut palms waving in the breeze.

"And my lucky day, too," added Mr. Buwaya, winking slyly. His mouth watered at the thought of fried monkey's liver served on a platter with garlic and onions.

Soon the crocodile was swimming, *whoosh, whoosh, whoosh,*

towards the other side of the river. Traffic was smooth as the fish darted out of his way. "I love to go sailing on days like this," he remarked. Then he sang his favorite song: "*Bu-bu-bu-wa-ya blues... No-no-no-need for shoes....*" Mr. Unggoy joined him in a duet.

When they were halfway across the river, Mr. Buwaya suddenly turned his face to Mr. Unggoy and said: "I need a monkey's liver for supper. And I want it now."

He grinned widely, *weh-eh-eh*, showing his dagger-sharp teeth and a cavernous mouth.

Mr. Unggoy turned cold with fear, *brr-r-r-r*, and his fur stood on end. He looked at the deep water around him. He was sorry he had not learned to swim when his father had tried to teach him. Now he was in danger of losing his one and only liver.

"Why, you should have told me earlier," said Mr. Unggoy, trying to sound calm although his teeth were chattering, *d-d-d-d-d*. "I left my liver hanging on the acacia tree back there. We monkeys like to hang our livers to dry on the branches of trees. I remember seeing several livers hanging beside mine."

He pointed to the river bank from where he had started on this dangerous voyage. Luckily, Mr. Buwaya's skin was too thick and scaly to feel Mr. Unggoy's trembling, *br-r-r-r, d-d-d-d*.

The crocodile's ears perked up at the sound of "livers." "*Tra-la-la*," he sang softly. How nice. He would surprise his wife with more than one liver for this evening's supper.

"I'll take you back home," Mr. Buwaya offered. "Then you can get me the livers."

"Sure!" spoke Mr. Unggoy. "Make it quick before my friends get there!"

Mr. Buwaya turned around and went full speed ahead, *zowee!* As soon as they were near enough, Mr. Unggoy leaped to shore, *zoot, zoot,* and scrambled up the nearest acacia tree.

Mr. Buwaya didn't see a single liver hanging on the branches of the tree. "Where are the livers you promised me?" he demanded.

"*Hee, hee, hee!*" chuckled Mr. Unggoy from behind the acacia leaves. "If you want a monkey's liver, come up and get it yourself! Here's my basket!" He dropped the empty basket on the ground, *bu-dong.*

Mr. Buwaya gnashed his teeth in anger, *grr-r-rit, grr-r-rit, grr-r-rit.* "I'm a fool!" he growled to himself. To Mr. Unggoy he shouted, "Some day I'll get you!"

"Bye-bye and good luck!" laughed Mr. Unggoy, watching Mr. Buwaya set sail for the mangrove swamp.

As Mr. Buwaya paddled home wearily, he could almost hear his wife's nagging voice: "What? No monkey's liver? Are we going to have river frogs again tonight?"

And she would whack him with her long tail.

The Ink Spouts

Bathala made the world millions of years ago. He made the sky, the sun and the moon, and all the other heavenly bodies. He made the forests, mountains, valleys, oceans, lakes, and rivers.

Bathala filled this beautiful planet with people and animals. Every time he finished making a group of animals, he called them to a meeting and told them what kind of work they should do.

When Bathala finished creating the water animals, he invited them to meet him at the bottom of the sea. "I am going to choose the officers of the Dagat-Ilog Society," he announced. "The members of this society will consist of all creatures who live in water."

On the day of the meeting, the water creatures hurried to the underwater hall where Bathala was waiting. Marine animals, such as Lobster, Dolphin, and Blue Marlin, swam from the far corners of the ocean to attend the meeting. Others, such as Milkfish, Catfish, and Tilapia, traveled a long way from lakes, ponds, and rivers. They were all eager to learn what they could do for the world they lived in.

Bathala looked very grand and powerful. He was sitting on a throne of pink coral and golden clam shells. His floor was strewn with pretty starfish and sea anemones. Seahorses guarded his throne, and electric eels made flashing lights in the water. Flying fish blew yellow and orange bubbles that looked like a million pearly balloons.

"Hail, Bathala! We have come to do your bidding!" chanted the water citizens. *Burble, gurgle, burble, gurgle*—their voices echoed throughout the vast ocean.

"Welcome!" answered Bathala. Then he called the roll, and his subjects answered, "Present!" Only two water animals were not there— Squid and Cuttlefish.

"Let us give them thirty minutes to arrive," said Bathala patiently.

The Dagat-Ilog society waited and waited. After thirty minutes, Bathala said, "The meeting will come to order." He brought out a long list of duties.

"I will make Stingray sergeant-at-arms," proclaimed Bathala, handing Stingray a piece of paper telling him what he should do. Since that day, Stingray has had a tail that looks like a whip.

"What shall I be?" asked Crab eagerly.

"A brave soldier," said Bathala. Since then, Crab has had large, strong forelegs that can grip and crush his enemy.

Before Bathala could finish passing out assignments, Squid and

Cuttlefish swam into view. They didn't seem to be in a hurry.

"Where have you have been?" asked Bathala sternly.

"Just floating around," answered the latecomers.

Bathala was quite angry. "You should have come on time," he scolded. "You kept the Dagat-Ilog Society waiting for half an hour."

"Now that we're here, give us the jobs we deserve," said Squid.

"Sit down and wait your turn," ordered Bathala. "Latecomers have no right to make demands."

Squid and Cuttlefish were embarrassed to be scolded in front of the other water animals. They wanted to get back at Bathala. So they swam to a corner behind some seaweeds to plot revenge.

"He has no right to talk to us like that," grumbled Cuttlefish.

"I know how we can spoil everybody's fun," whispered Squid. "Let's throw mud at Bathala's papers."

Cuttlefish agreed that it would be a joy to make a mess. So they scooped up the blackest mud they could find on the floor of the sea. Then they returned to the meeting.

With their tentacles Squid and Cuttleflish hurled mudballs at the papers of the other water creatures. They also made a muddy mess of the other papers Bathala was holding.

"*Di-ri di-ri!*" screamed Stingray, trying to whip Cuttlefish with his tail. Crab tried to grab Squid with his curved claws, but Squid swam away too fast, *quee, quee, quee*.

The other sea animals darted away to avoid the mud. The seahorses hid behind Bathala. The electric eels couldn't make lights because they were blinded by the mud in their eyes, *eee, eee, eee!*

Milkfish, Catfish, and Tilapia searched for the nearest exit so they could swim to their fresh-water home.

Bathala rose from his throne and pointed his forefinger at Squid and Cuttlefish. "You two!" he thundered. "You'll be sorry for this! From now on you will each carry a pouch of black mud! You will move very slowly because your load will weigh you down."

Squid was sorry he had been so naughty. "Please spare me!" he pleaded with Bathala. "I won't do it again."

But Bathala showed him no mercy. Instead he added another punishment. "You and your children will never grow to the size of Octopus," he said to Squid. "You will all stay as small as you are today."

Since the time they angered Bathala, Squid and Cuttlefish have been squirting inky mud from their pouches, *prrit, prrit, prrit*, whether they want to or not. The other marine animals avoid them because they don't want to be spattered with dirty ink. "*Eek, eek!* Here come the ink spouts!" they shout when Squid and Cuttlefish happen to stray into their neighborhood.

The Lonesome Snail

Long, long ago, shortly after Bathala made the world, different kinds of animals lived together like one happy family.

Among the animals who decided to live together were Dalag the mudfish, Tutubi the dragonfly, Putakti the wasp, and Kuhol the snail. They lived in a cozy little house by a tinkling brook. Around the house were vines and water plants that shaded them from the sun.

The four friends divided the housework among themselves, depending on what each could do best. Tutubi, Putakti, and Kuhol asked Dalag to be the head of the household.

"You are the biggest," they told the mudfish. "So you should be our leader and make the important decisions."

"All right," replied Dalag. "I will run the household and find food for us to eat. But each of you must have a job to do. What would you like to be, Tutubi?"

The dragonfly fluttered his delicate wings and hummed, "I can be a messenger because I can fly the fastest."

"Good," said Dalag. "Now who will guard the house?"

"I will be the guard," buzzed the wasp. "My sting can poison anyone who tries to break in."

"Wonderful," said Dalag. "Now, Kuhol, what can you do for the household?"

"I'm too slow to run errands but I can be the cook. I can also keep the house clean," answered Kuhol, nodding her little antennae.

The four friends did their best to make the household run smoothly. They worked well together. Dalag brought home tadpoles and vegetables, and Kuhol cooked yummy dishes three times a day.

Tutubi brought news about the weather. He told his friends when the sun would be out and when it would rain.

Putakti was a brave and watchful guard. Snakes could not come near the house for fear of getting stung. Putakti also repaired the house because he could carry bits of soil to patch the holes each time the roof leaked.

The four friends lived together this way and were very happy.

Early one morning Dalag was swimming in the brook looking for food. Suddenly he spied something wriggling in the water. As he got closer, he saw a worm caught among the weeds.

"Here's lunch!" said Dalag.

Without thinking twice, he seized the worm with his mouth and began to swim home. Little did he know that there was a hook sticking out of the worm's belly. The hook was tied to the end of a fishing line.

Dalag soon felt the hook piercing his own mouth. *Aray, aray!* He felt something pulling him to the surface of the water. Suddenly he couldn't swim anymore. He could only shake his body. He tried to spit out the worm but the hook held fast. Before he knew it, a fisherman had caught him and put him in his basket. Then he brought the mudfish home. Dalag was never heard from again.

Tutubi, Putakti, and Kuhol waited all day for Dalag to come home. He had never been late before. They were hungry and worried.

The next day Tutubi told his friends, "Let me go look for Dalag."

He got ready to leave but before he did, he decided to fix his necktie so it would fit snugly. The dragonfly flew off, *hum, hum, hum,* to search for Dalag. He flew to the rice paddies but there was no sign of the missing mudfish. He hovered over the brook, looking into the water to see if his friend was swimming among other fish.

Then he saw a fish named Bolasi, whose lips moved in a strange way when his head was out of the water. "*Glub, glub,*" Bolasi seemed to be saying with his funny lips.

Tutubi thought Bolasi was laughing at him. "Why are you laughing?" asked Tutubi. "Is my necktie too loose?"

"*Glub, glub,*" went Bolasi's lips.

"*Zzzit-zit,* stop laughing at my necktie," warned Tutubi, "or I shall call Putakti to sting you." He tightened his necktie a little more.

Bolasi continued to say, "*Glub, glub.*"

Tutubi tightened his necktie once again. *Ouch, ouch!* The necktie became so tight that Tutubi started to choke. That was the last time he was seen alive.

After two days of waiting, Putakti and Kuhol were more worried than ever. They were also very hungry, for even if Kuhol knew how to cook, there was no food in the kitchen. Luckily for Kuhol, she could eat a little mud while waiting for better food. Putakti, however, could only tighten his belt so he wouldn't feel hunger pangs.

"I'd better go find Dalag and Tutubi," said Putakti on the third day.

So Putakti flew out, *buzz, buzz,* in search of his two friends.

"Dalag! Tutubi!" he called out.

Salagubang the beetle and Salaginto the goldbug came out of their homes as soon as they heard the wasp buzzing.

"Have you seen Dalag and Tutubi?" he asked.

Salagubang answered, "We saw Tutubi the other day. He was talking to Bolasi in the brook."

Putakti buzzed his way towards the brook. He felt sure he would come upon Dalag and Tutubi on their way home.

But Putakti got hungrier and hungrier as he flew, and his tummy got thinner and thinner. He kept tightening his belt to stop the hunger pangs. At last he tightened it so hard that his body broke in two. That was the end of Putakti.

Kuhol was now all alone in the house. After a week, she was so lonely that she could not stand it any longer. She began to weep, "*Waa-laa, waa-laa.*" Then she set out to find her friends.

Kuhol asked Palaka the frog, Butiki the lizard, and Daga the mouse to help her but they only looked puzzled. She searched among the

bushes and the water lilies. She wandered in the rice fields and the sugarcane fields. At night Alitaptap the firefly tried to help by lighting the way.

Whenever Kuhol saw a blade of grass or a *palay* stalk, she would climb to the top and look as far as she could see. Her little antennae would point back and forth, left and right, up and down. Swaying with the grass, she would weep softly, *"Waa-laa, waa-laa."*

Even today you can still see Kuhol creeping up blades of grass and stems of plants, sobbing and searching for her friends.

The Hawk's Rubies

O f all the birds that roamed the skies, Hawk was the vainest. It was not enough that he had strength and power. He also wanted to be the handsomest. He wished he had the silky blue feathers of Fairy Bluebird, and the yellow breast of Forest Kingfisher, and the bright green tail of Parrot-Finch.

One morning, while Hawk was perched on the branch of a molave tree wondering how he could make himself more handsome, he saw a merchant walking by. The man was carrying a small bag.

"What do you have there?" Hawk called out.

"Jewels!" answered the man. "I'm a jeweler. Would you like to see what's in my bag?"

"Why not?" Hawk answered, hopping off the tree.

The jeweler pulled out a velvet box from the bag and opened it.

"Bee-yoo-ti-ful!" screeched Hawk when he saw the dazzling jewels on display.

There were pink and white diamond necklaces with matching rings and earrings. There were gleaming gold and silver bracelets, and shiny nose rings, too. All the jewels were fit for a queen to wear.

"Take your pick," said the man.

Hawk put on a pearl bracelet. He liked it very much but it hung loosely on his wrist.

"I can't wear a bracelet," he said. "It will surely fall off when I fly." He tried an emerald ring but it didn't fit on any of his long talons. *"Uh uh uh,* too tight," he complained.

"You can't wear earrings because your ear lobes are too tiny," observed the jeweler. "But you can wear a necklace without losing it."

Hawk agreed that he could carry a necklace very well because he always held his head up high.

There were three necklaces to choose from. One was made of diamonds, another of rubies, and another of gold beads.

"I want the most expensive necklace," said Hawk. "I want to be the best-dressed bird in the kingdom."

"Take the rubies then," said the jeweler. "See how they sparkle like red stars beside your jet-black eyes?"

Hawk felt very handsome indeed. He bought the ruby necklace and wore it around his neck with great pride. Bluebird, Kingfisher, and Parrot-Finch gazed at him with envy. Mynah Bird piped, *"Po-gee, po-gee!"*

A few kilometers from Hawk's nest was a wide and shady barnyard which he visited quite often. Some of his feathered friends lived there. Now that he had a new necklace, he wanted to show it off to them.

So he flew back and forth above the barnyard, flapping his large wings—*prap-prap-prap-prap*—to attract attention before landing on the ground.

At the sight of Hawk's sparkling red stones, Hen came running to greet him. She was followed by her seven fluffy chicks.

"*Cluck, cluck, cluck!* What a gorgeous necklace!" cried Hen. "May I borrow it? I have nothing to wear to the barnyard ball tonight."

"Yes, you may," answered Hawk, who liked the hen. "But only for tonight."

Hawk was in a generous mood. He had never felt so good in his life. And he was pleased to see Rooster giving him a jealous look as he chatted with Hen.

Hawk slipped off the necklace and put it around Hen's neck. She strutted round and round, preening her feathers. The chicks went "*Cheep, cheep, cheep!*" when they saw their pretty mother. "Now Mama can go to the barnyard ball!"

"I'll be back at sunrise tomorrow," said Hawk. "Take good care of my necklace."

And Hawk flew off, *prap, prap,* to his nest on the cliff.

Early the next morning Hawk heard Rooster crowing from far away, *"Tar-tar-a-ok! Tar-tar-a-ok!"*

"Time to get my necklace," said Hawk, stretching himself with a yawn. He took off from his cliff and swooped down to the barnyard.

At first there was a mysterious quiet in the yard. Hawk sat on a fence and looked around suspiciously. Not a hen or a chick could he see.

Then he noticed Duck and Goose waddling out of the barn, followed by Turkey. "*Quack, quack, quack,*" said Duck to Goose. "*Honk, honk,*" said Goose to Duck. Turkey interrupted with "*Gaggle, gaggle, gaggle.*" They all sounded worried about something.

Then Hawk heard Pigeon and Rice Bird whispering to one another as they hopped and fluttered in the branches of the camachile tree. "*Peep, peep, tweet, tweet,*" they chirped softly. They, too, sounded nervous.

Finally, Hen and her chicks came clucking and cheeping out of the hen house. To Hawk's astonishment, Hen's neck was bare.

"Where is my necklace?" he demanded. His jet-black eyes glowed like two coals of fire.

"It's lost!" replied Hen timidly. "My children took it while I was asleep, and they can't remember where they put it. We've been looking *all over* for it!"

"How careless can you get!" snapped Hawk in anger. "You must pay for my necklace right away! If you don't, I'll have you arrested for stealing!"

Hen was so frightened she began to cry. She had no money to pay for the necklace. Nor could she sell any eggs because they had all hatched.

All the barnyard birds felt sorry for Hen. "She's such a sweet chicken, and a good mother, too," cooed Pigeon, hoping to soften Hawk's hard heart.

But Hawk was getting impatient. He was on his way to a fiesta where he had hoped to show off his gems. He spoke sharply: "Hen, I will take one of your chicks every day in exchange for what you owe me. When you give me back my necklace, I'll stop taking your chicks."

"*Cheep, cheep, cheep!*" cried the poor chicks, scurrying in circles to escape Hawk's clutches. But he caught one of them with his huge talons. Then he zoomed up to the sky.

"My baby!" screamed Hen.

But Hawk and chick had vanished.

Hen gathered the rest of her children under her wings. "Mama, we'll help you find the necklace," they promised. "It must be somewhere in the yard."

To this day you can see Hen and her chicks, their heads to the ground, looking for the lost necklace. Scratch, scratch, *tuka, tuka*.... Scratch, scratch, *tuka, tuka*....day in and day out. They will never stop until they find the lost rubies.

And Hawk will never stop snatching tiny chicks until he gets back his precious necklace.

The Cattle's New Clothes

A long time ago, Cow and Carabao looked different from the way they do today. Cow wore a black suit and Carabao wore a brown suit.

Cow and Carabao were close friends because they worked together on a farm. All day long they plowed the rice fields under the blazing sun. They pulled heavy carts loaded with firewood and sacks of grain. Although Cow was smaller than Carabao, they both worked very hard.

Their master, Mang Damot, a stingy farmer, never paid Cow and Carabao for their back-breaking work. Instead he would beat them with a long stick when they did not move fast enough for him. Worst of all, he refused to give them a bath.

Carabao could not stand his own smell. "*Ugh ugh!* Do I smell like a pigsty?" he wondered.

"*Hmf, hmf,* I'm afraid you do," answered Cow, sniffing the air.

"And so do you," Carabao said, also sniffing.

One morning Cow woke up with a high fever. He felt as if he were lying on a bed of charcoal. Carabao tried to cool Cow by fanning him with a large palm leaf. But the fever wouldn't go down.

"I'm tired of working myself to the bone," wailed Cow. "I'm tired of getting beaten and starved. I'm tired of going bathless day after day."

"Let's run away when you feel better," suggested Carabao.

"Yes," said Cow excitedly. "Let's leave Mang Damot to plow the field all by himself."

After two weeks Cow's fever was gone. It was time for the two friends to plan their escape.

"We must wait for a dark night," whispered Carabao, "with no moon and stars to light the earth."

But he was worried about getting out of the yard where the farmer kept all his animals. The yard was surrounded by a bamboo fence which was too high to jump over.

"I know what," whispered Cow. "Let's break down one corner of the fence little by little."

They chose a part of the fence which was hidden by trees and bushes. Every afternoon, while the farmer was napping in his nipa hut, Cow and Carabao would take turns at the fence. Cow would nibble away at the bamboo quietly, bit by bit, *geet, geet, geet.* Then he would rest while Carabao did his share of nibbling, *gut, gut, gut.* It took them five days to tear down a part of the fence big enough to let the pair through.

At last the right night came. The moon and stars were covered by dark clouds. While the farmer snored loudly, *z-z-z-z*, in his nipa hut, Cow and Carabao crawled through the hole in the fence. They escaped from the farm, running as fast as their hooves could carry them, *tig-i-dag, tig-i-dag, tig-i-dag*.

When the sun rose the next morning, they thought they were far enough from their cruel master. They were very tired and could hardly keep their eyes open from lack of sleep. As they plodded on, the sun's rays beat down on their sweating bodies.

After several hours, they were delighted to come upon a pond of clear water.

Cow asked, "What shall we do first—take a nap or take a bath?"

Carabao was more eager to look and smell clean. "Bath first!" he said.

The two friends stripped off their clothes and jumped into the pond. It was cool and refreshing.

"*Mmmooo-oo-oo,*" murmured Cow. She was neck-deep in the gently swirling water.

"*Maw-uff, maw-uff,* I like this!" grunted Carabao with satisfaction. He splashed water onto his back with his tail, *swish, swish, swish*.

Suddenly they heard a familiar voice from far away, a voice they feared and hated. It was their master coming over the hill, shaking his stick wildly in the wind.

"Come back here! Come back, you good-for-nothing cattle!" shouted Mang Damot furiously.

Before the farmer reached the pond, Cow and Carabao clambered out of the water. They got dressed in a hurry. Cow ran to the left, Carabao ran to the right. The farmer just stood there, not knowing which way to go.

Carabao ran for about half an hour before stopping to rest in a bamboo grove. He had never been so tired. He found himself sweating more than usual, *drip, drip, drip*. Only then did he notice that his suit felt awfully tight, especially around the neck.

Nearby, he saw another pond of clear water. He huffed and puffed his way towards the pond, not to take another bath—for he feared the farmer would catch up with him—but to have a drink of water.

As Carabao bent his head to drink, he saw his reflection in the pond. Surprise! He was not dressed in his old brown suit anymore. He was dressed in glossy black!

"Maw-aw-aw!" exclaimed Carabao. "This is Cow's suit, not mine!"

Meantime, Cow was dragging his weary body, *kadadang, kadadang*, to the shade of a mango tree. He was afraid of catching a fever again. However, even though he was very tired, he did not feel the heat too much. A soft breeze was touching his neck.

Then he found out why his neck felt cool. His collar was so loose that it dangled like a short curtain beneath his neck. And his collar was not black anymore, but brown! He looked at his suit and noticed that it was brown all over!

"Moo-oo-eee!" exclaimed Cow in surprise. "I took Carabao's suit by mistake!"

The two friends never changed into each other's clothes for they never met again.

And that is why, to this day, Carabao has tight black skin and Cow has loose brown skin. Carabao often wallows in ponds and shallow rivers because he wants to cool off. Cow has grown to like the new skin hanging in folds from his neck. You'll often find him grazing happily in green pastures.

Sources of the Stories

The stories in this book were taken from the book *Filipino Popular Tales*, Collected and Edited, with Comparative Notes, by Dean S. Fansler, Ph.D. (Lancaster, Pa. and New York: The American Folk-Lore Society, 1921).

The Stories:

"The Carabao-Turtle Race" is retold from "An Unequal Match; or, Why the Carabao's Hoof is Split." Narrated by Godofredo Rivera of Pagsanjan, Laguna. (Pp. 428-29.)

"How Pagong Made a Fool of Matsing" is retold from "The Turtle and the Monkey." Narrated by Eutiquiano Garcia of Mexico, Pampanga. (Pp. 366-67.)

"The Bird that Reached the Sun" is retold from "The Hawk and the Coling." Narrated by Agapito Gaa of Taal, Batangas. (Pp. 408-09.)

"Mr. Buwaya and Mr. Unggoy" is retold from "The Monkey and the Crocodile." Narrated by Engracio Abasola of Manila. (Pp. 374-75.)

"The Ink Spouts" is retold from "Why the Cuttlefish and Squid Produce a Black Liquid." Narrated by Victoria Ciudadano of Batangas. (Pp. 419-20.)

"The Lonesome Snail" is retold from "Why Snails Climb Up Grass." Narrated by Jose E. Tomeldan of Binalonan, Pangasinan. (Pp. 417-18.)

"The Hawk's Rubies" is retold from "The Lost Necklace." Narrated by Facundo Esquivel, a Tagalog who heard it from a Cebuano. (Pp. 414-15.)

"The Cattle's New Clothes" is retold from "Why the Cow's Skin is Loose on the Neck." Narrated by Francisco M. Africa (no province given, but another version was told by a Tagalog from Mindoro.) (Pp. 410-11.)

For Further Reading

Philippine Folk Literature: THE FOLKTALES, Compiled and Edited by Damiana L. Eugenio (Quezon City, Philippines: U.P. Folklorists, Inc., U.P. Diliman, in cooperation with the Philippine National Science Society, 1989).

Philippine Folk Literature: THE MYTHS, Compiled and Edited by Damiana L. Eugenio (Quezon City, Philippines: University of the Philippines Press, 1993).

La Fontaine's Fables (London: Everyman's Library; New York: Dutton, 1952).

Aesop Without Morals: The Famous Fables and a Life of Aesop, newly translated by Lloyd W. Daly (New York: Thomas Yoseloff, Publisher, 1961).

About the Author

Sylvia Mendez Ventura graduated with degrees in English from Barnard College and Columbia University. In addition to dozens of book reviews and articles, she has written fables and children's stories. Her story "The Tangerine Gumamela" won second prize in the Carlos Palanca Memorial Awards for The Short Story (English division) in 1984. *Jose Rizal,* her first biography for Tahanan Books for Young Readers' Great Lives series, was praised by *The Philippine Star* as "a remarkable book about the most remarkable Filipino who ever lived....to put so many details in so short a book is a marvelous achievement." Her most recent book for adults is *Ragtime in Kamuning: Sari-sari Essays,* for which she was voted National Fellow for the Essay (1993-1994) by the U.P. Creative Writing Center.

Ms. Ventura teaches English and comparative literature at the University of the Philippines and is currently director of the University of the Philippines Press.

The author lives with her husband, Constante Ventura, in Quezon City.

About the Artist

Joanne de León was born in Baguio City. She has a bachelor's degree in fine arts from the University of the Philippines (Diliman), where she majored in painting. In 1990 she received the grand prize for best children's book illustration from the Philippine Board on Books for Young People. Her book *Ang Nawawalang Araw* won a prize at the 1992 Noma Concours for Picture Book Illustrations contest, sponsored by the Asian Cultural Centre for UNESCO. Among the picture books she has illustrated are *The Environmental Alphabet* and *Pinatubo, the Planted Mountain.*

Ms. de León is a member of Ang Ilustrador ng Kabataan (INK), an organization of young artists devoted to children's book illustration. She lives in Diliman, Quezon City.